FIRST DAY AT WORK

Journey of a woman through the
prisons of pattern

DEBASIS BHAUMIK

ISBN

Paperback 979-8-89744-295-9
Hardcase 979-8-89984-263-4

A must-read for all women and everyone
else who considers themselves an ally

Dedicated to:

Uma and a billion other women in this world who fight every day to break free from societal patterns

Contents

Acknowledgement

My wife who always tolerates (almost encourages) all my new projects and supports me in whatever way she can. My son, Rishi Bhaumik, who is also the first-round reviewer of this book.

Introduction

The world is constantly changing, shattering old and establishing new patterns. In the process, and to make progress, there is conflict. Innovation, then, is a revolution, forcibly dividing the faithful from the visionaries, the obedient from the creative.

This is a book based on the journey of a woman who dared to challenge the status quo to create a fascinating world of opportunities for her family. She faced cultural norms and doubted her future. Facing fierce family disagreements, she constantly wondered how she could possibly break the long-established patterns.

We live in a very interesting world today. We always have a constant inflow of new inventions, which is causing lifestyle changes. We have at least one standing war or political crisis going on in some part of the world at all times. We have an extremely smart generation who are always looking down at their extended self on their smartphone or tablet.

We might wonder, is this a new pattern in working?

Gone are the days when everyone waited for the paper newspaper in the morning; we are fed with news bytes twenty-four-seven. We expect to know everything right away. We do not care as much about show times on television; we want to be entertained in our own way, on our own time, except for a few live events like the Super Bowl.

Major stock markets are going up cumulatively year over year as if the bull can't stop running. Power in the hands of major fund managers is more than ever before. Their influence is reaching far beyond finance. When environmental metrics became important to the funds, all corporations and hence, society started to put way more focus and investments on the topic. As I am writing the book, momentum is definitely slowing down for the investors; as a result, society is also becoming lukewarm to the climate focus.

Artificial intelligence (AI) is making news every day in the media, which makes some very nervous and some extremely excited about the future. For me, the excitement is way more than the risks. I'm looking forward to this new pattern.

In the last few industrial revolutions, the impact was more on the frontline of production, which is practically fully automated in most industries today. In the past rounds, knowledge-based professions were not impacted as much. AI has the potential not only to further automate and optimise production lines and well-scripted processes but also to impact the basic premises of knowledge-based professions. AI might as well take on more decision-making work than humans, improving overall decision quality.

Maybe I am too optimistic. I believe that based on all the innovations enabled by technology, including AI, we will reach a different state of abundance in society. It truly excites me. I know abundance sounds a little too far-fetched when two and a half billion people in the world are still living with food insecurity. But I believe it will come. Like many other life-threatening diseases, we will be able to eradicate 'food insecurity'.

My personal wish is to see that happen in my lifetime.

We talk about generative Artificial Intelligence (AI) all over social media, personalised micronutrition for healthy living, more women on corporate boards or corporations, and many such changes. Innovation in Agriculture and food production. All sounds very positive to me in various ways. That's why I believe abundance is on the horizon for humanity.

Though AI will make significant progress, at least for the next few decades, humans will be leading the journey to abundance. To make the right evolution for humans, it is important we engage the bright minds to lead us. Not to get biased by gender at birth. The need for human leadership has never been as crucial. Lots at stake.

I am personally involved with an awesome social organisation where we promote and support STEM (Science, Technology, Engineering, Maths) education across Canada, including girls and children at remote locations in our very vast country. Love the results and the success stories. I know that STEM will create that pipeline for progress through the application of science. And will include those smart young girls to contribute to this journey.

In our family, my awesome niece is one of the finest curious minds, getting ready for her engineering. She is in grade eleven now and is super clear about which engineering speciality she wants to pursue at university. I have zero doubt that she will be successful with her plans and will bring a lot of goodness to this world. She is just hardworking, independent and bright.

I feel she is not held back by patterns.

Last year, around this time, I got to stay at a very fancy hotel for the weekend, with food, drinks, and activities paid for in the heart of Banff National Park, one of the most beautiful places in the world. All of that was courtesy of my wife. She received the President's League Award. It was their organisation's own reward system for exceptional performers. Her photo went on their corporate office wall, kind of like a hall of fame. I am so proud of her.

I love it when talent gets to express itself and is not constrained by gender at birth. I get encouraged by my wife, my niece, Brené Brown, Michelle Obama, Sheryl Sandberg, and most importantly, all my amazing female coworkers.

Then I hear on the news that in some parts of the world, men are deciding on women's code of conduct in public. What can she be allowed to talk about? What can she wear? Is she even allowed to speak outside of the home?

It becomes news when some parts of the world now allow women to drive and get a driver's licence. Really?

Give? Allow? Who gave us the right to 'Give', the right to 'Allow'?

Are we going backwards?

I was having a conversation about the above examples with one of my professional friends, Susan (not the original name), who said, "Yeah, the situation is so bad in those countries."

I was not surprised that Susan said that. That's what we choose to believe in the western part of the world. That we are perfect, or at least good enough. It is the women in the Middle East or the eastern part of the world who have problems.

I said to Susan, "How is it different from us in the western world?" Susan was surprised and replied, "What do you mean?"

I meant it is no different from a bunch of older men doing politics around women's right to abortion.

Susan took a pause. A long one.

You can argue that this is different. But you will not convince me of that.

Are we really making progress, or are societal patterns holding us back?

This is a book based on the life of a woman who was born in India a month before India's independence in August 1947 and her journey of almost eight decades. A story which moves through societal patterns and observations.

The book talks about Uma's relentless efforts to fight the norm, her submissions, and her acceptance.

Uma had a very simple dream. She wanted to be a teacher and a lifelong learner and stay surrounded by books. This book explores whether Uma achieves her dream and the price she pays along the way as she tries.

Uma is not just an Indian woman in her seventies; she represents billions of women around the world, from east to west and north to south.

Busy Morning

Sunday evening, just after supper, on a pleasant day in August. A beautiful sunny summer day in Calgary. I was sitting on the patio in my green backyard all by myself. Just soaking in everything going on. It was a good busy day. Went for a sixty-kilometre bike ride by myself in the morning. After I returned, my family and I went for a walk and enjoyed paddle boating. My niece joined us. We consider her a daughter. Had good food by the Bow River. That's my kind of great weekend. Love summer in Calgary.

I was watching the higher traffic volume of planes taking off from Calgary Airport, which is about eight kilometres from our house. Our backyard is at such an angle that we can see all incoming and outgoing flights once they are a few thousand feet from the ground. We are just close enough to get the view and far enough not to hear the sound as much. I like watching flights going up and down. The view somehow takes my mind to places.

Every flight is like hundreds of humans going towards or away from their goals, dreams and folks. Each one of them is a living story. Each one has so many more connected to them through the strings of family and other emotional connections. And those folks are also connected to a few more through genetics, emotions, beliefs, faith and nationality. As my mind wandered around, I remembered my little boy asking me a few years back, "What is quantum entanglement?" I think he was about nine years old around that time. He saw something on the internet about the Nobel Prize in Physics that year, and he saw that word in the title. I was not sure how to explain to a nine-year-old. I said, "When I was travelling earlier in the year to another country and you had a cut on your leg and you called me crying, I felt the pain as well, though I was physically away and was hurt myself." I paused. He said, "Oh, I see."

I travel more than once a month for work. I have designated pouches for all the things I need. All of them are pretty much set in the suitcase. Just add in a couple of shirts, trousers, and refill the pouches with fresh underwear, and I am set to go. Of course, this is not special. Most people travelling for work have the same script. Ubers or rental cars for the first and last mile.

But one thing catches my eye every time. There are always some people waiting to receive some of the travellers at the airport. Some are in black shirts and jackets with name tags on. I am not talking about them. They are there for business travellers. I am talking about the families who come to see off or receive their loved ones. I look into their eyes. Some are wet with happiness and some with sadness. Funny how our eyes get moist both on happy and sad occasions.

Sunday is the busiest day at Calgary airport. I learned that information a few years back. My son and I went for a par-three golf round. They paired us with a lovely young couple. We started socialising between the shots. The lady worked with a local airline company as part of their ground crew. It was a Sunday. As the planes were taking off one after the other over the golf course, she mentioned, "Sunday is the busiest day at the airport." I asked, "Why Sunday?" She said, "Most people travel on Sunday night for work so that they can be at their destination

Monday morning." I guess that makes sense; I learned something new.

While I was soaking in the sun, the planes reminded me of Uma. Uma must be getting ready for Monday right now, as it is already Monday morning in India. I decided to call her to pass on my best wishes for the day. To be honest, I have been missing Uma for the last few weeks. I am often not the best at expressing my emotions. I did not share that feeling with her or anyone else. My professional coach often encourages me to articulate and more often share my emotions towards my people, my family, my team, and my friends. I have been recently practising verbalising my emotions to my discomfort. For what it's worth, it feels nice, and I strongly encourage all my introverted readers to express their authentic emotions more. You will feel good, and so will your folks. My eleven-year-old says, "I love you, mom," a hundred times a day. I think it is way too many, as I do not even get one-fourth of that in a week. The reality is I do not express my love for my mom as frequently as I should, either.

I decided to call Uma. The phone rang. Malti picked up. Malti has been with Uma for the last forty years. Malti came as a very young single mom looking for a place to live in exchange for house help work. Uma hired her and she stayed back for four decades. She took care of household chores and had a big part in raising Uma's kids and grandkids. Some of the kids could not even pronounce 'Malti' when they started interacting with her. They often called her something else. For example, Uma's daughter called her 'Balti' and kept calling her that even now when she is grown up and a mother of one herself. Balti is a grandma now too. Malti lives in one of the many rooms in the house. She gets up every day before anyone else and keeps working in the kitchen, cleaning, washing clothes, giving oil massages to Uma, and so on. There is nothing out of scope for her job description.

"Uma mam is in the bathroom; she is getting ready," Malti said. I said, "That's fine, nothing urgent. I will call her at the end of her Monday and my Monday morning. How are you?" Malti replied, "I am always good." I acknowledged the reply with a gentle laugh and hung up.

I went to the kitchen and made chamomile tea for myself, then came back and sat down in the deck chair. Long sunny evenings are a privilege. We enjoy around ninety to a hundred such days a year in this part of the world. I try to spend as much time outside as I can during these months.

While sipping my tea slowly, I was thinking about Uma. I did not make it to India to attend the funeral of her husband last week. I knew she would have liked it. I am not sure why I did not. Somehow, I tend to avoid participation in elaborate East Indian funerals. I find they are too busy and extensive, and I struggle to connect back with the person in focus. Maybe I did not want to get myself wrapped up in many other emotions that come up for me when I am in India. Not sure. The fact remains Uma expected me to show up, and I did not.

A few years ago, my dad passed away. He had lung cancer and was diagnosed at the fourth stage. I went and saw him for the last time. It was different. This was the first time in decades that there was no one waiting for me at the Kolkata airport. My dad came every time. I mean every time I landed at that airport. Obviously, he was not in a state to leave the house at that time. I took a taxi and reached home. He was not waiting with his ever-honest smile of joy and a big hug. A hug of unconditional love. Each hug always said to me that he loved me despite all the troubles I had brought him during my high school and college days.

It was heartbreaking to see him in excruciating pain coming out of chemo. I have seen him ill a few times growing up. They were very short-lived. Through all that, he was positive and had the same energy. His energy never went down. As a little boy, I had chicken pox. For twenty-one days, he took time off from work and became my caregiver by choice. He did everything for me, including reading an enormous number of books. The idea was to isolate me from my baby sister and others in the family. He isolated with me.

I struggled a lot seeing him in pain. A visual I have never seen before where my dad is losing to the disease. I think it was more painful to see my pillar of trust crashing in front of me. I guess that's the circle of life. I went and spent as much time as I could and then came back. I could not do even close to what he did for me every time I was under the weather growing up. My sister was the stronger one, and she quarterbacked all those months. Anyone who had parents with terminal diseases would know it is at least as hard on the caregiver.

My sister called over the long weekend of September, only a few weeks after I came back and said that my dad was no more. I never experienced any pain deeper than that. I did his funeral in my way but didn't go back to participate in the rituals and host hundreds of invitees as per tradition. Till today, I am not sure it was the right decision.

Every year, on his birthday in December towards the end of the year, my family and I take toys, dry food items, and spend some time at a home that takes care of kids in need between the ages of two and nine. That's my way of celebrating his life. My son, who is eleven now, is not particularly excited about holding my hand while walking these days. But he somehow always holds my hand tighter on our way out of those kids' home up to the car. I am surely not suggesting anything to my readers about funerals and rituals. I just thought of sharing a little anecdote of my relationship with death.

Though I did not travel to be part of Uma's husband's funeral, I have been talking over the phone with her and her kids every day since the passing away of Uma's husband a few weeks back. Several times, Uma broke down over the phone talking about her loss. In between her sad spells, I heard conviction and pride. The pride that her husband led a life on his terms and passed away with dignity. They were together for just over fifty years. That's a long time, almost as long as I have been in this world.

Uma is an interesting person with very poor health but an immense amount of mental strength and courage. Uma was diagnosed with a rheumatic heart condition several years ago, which is now in an advanced stage and beyond surgery. She is on several pills multiple times a day. While I was worrying about her health and loneliness on becoming single after fifty years, several instances of her exceptional courage stories came to my mind, which gave me a bit more comfort.

It would have been good to hear her voice. But I can imagine the busyness and stress of a new day as a newly single person in the morning for her.

Uma's son and daughter and their family all live in Canada now. They went to attend the funeral in India. Their presence gave

Uma some company for the last few weeks. Today is just different as everyone left over the weekend, and today is a fresh start for Uma.

After fifty years of marriage, after the funeral, Uma is now living alone in their fairly large mansion, except for Malti. Uma lives in a very large house. The house came together organically over the years. It has six stories, twenty-three bathrooms, lots of rooms, an elevator, an office and a school. There is a remnant of a large factory across the street as well which was used for welding, parking several trucks, cars and a little garden for a party with swings. The house was not designed to be like this at the beginning. Over the years, as cash came in and there was the right opportunity, Uma's husband kept extending and building the house. Being an engineer himself, in combination with the construction business, made it easy.

It used to be a busy household where there were always lots of employees; visitors kept that whole street humming. There was not a time when someone was not cooking something in the kitchen for the family or guests.

There is not much business left. The primary business was around construction. Involved in highway construction, construction of government institutions and buildings, which later diversified to include the implementation of cell phone towers when it became a huge growth area. Over the last ten years, most of those businesses almost dried up for several reasons. The change of regime in the government, Uma's kid moving away abroad, and the declining health of Uma's husband are the more impactful ones.

The only thing that is still running is the kindergarten to grade five school. Uma did not let that change. Actually, the school has a good reputation and is doing very well with a waiting list for admission. Of late, Uma's husband was the principal and owner of the school. That's where he spent almost all his time. Uma joined him in the school's annual events like sports day, award night, and such.

There was a natural and practical consideration of downsizing and simplifying everything after her husband's death. One of the suggestions was to sell the school and the mansion. The practical approach would have been to sell the school, the remaining business, and the massive house and move to a smaller independent living apartment within a well-maintained, guarded community. This had actually been a point of discussion for the last several years for Uma's kids regarding the older couple. Uma never showed any interest in that topic and literally resented it whenever it came up.

Uma did not agree with any of that. Uma was not ready to downsize and be dependent. She was actually a bit upset whenever the topic came up. Uma decided to continue with life in the current form, in her current setting. There is a lot of pride and dignity associated with that for Uma.

A part of me is worried about Uma's health and her ability to run a school. In addition, Uma has never worked outside the home. She has been a full-time wife and mom. Her expertise in cooking and hosting is often discussed and talked of highly by family and friends. No one ever talked about Uma running a business or, for that matter, an educational institution. However, with Uma's husband passing away and kids out of the country, a lot fell on Uma to manage starting today.

I knew when I called that it would be a busy day for Uma. Will it be really busier than a typical day, though? Not sure. Uma's husband always woke up in the morning before 5 am. As a result, Uma hardly ever slept past that time. Uma's morning routine lately included an hour in the worship room, making breakfast and tea for her husband, getting clothes and everything ready in a very organised manner for him.

As soon as her husband left for the office and school, Uma started her lunch preparation. Lunch at Uma's place was never trivial. There is no concept of ready-to-eat or packaged food. Everything was elaborate, mostly made from scratch and served warm and fresh.

Hilsa fish is considered one of the most delicious fish in that part of the world. The fish is super tasty but is extremely bony. I am not a huge Hilsa fan. So, I always avoided Hilsa at Uma's place while everyone else really raved about it. One day, Uma noticed that and asked me why I avoided Hilsa. "Do you have an allergy?" Uma asked. It felt like getting caught by your middle school teacher for doing something you are not supposed to do. I said very politely, "It's too bony for me to enjoy the taste." She smiled and left without making me any more uncomfortable. From that day onwards, every time I was invited and there was Hilsa on the menu, they were prepared boneless, and bones were removed by hand. Trust me, boneless Hilsa is not common in any part of the world and at any stretch.

I have never seen Uma less busy in the morning. So, I am not sure what her new routine will be. Will it be busier and harder for her, or maybe the opposite? When her kids were young, the morning routine included dropping them at school too. Her kids have grown up and left long ago, yet somehow, she spent all her time around her husband and doing chores around the house. Maybe history will repeat itself, and Uma will be busy in the morning again with her new routine.

I was thinking about Uma's age for some reason. Uma's seventy-seventh birthday was in July 2024. I consider myself a thought leader in Diversity and Inclusion and have even written a book on this topic; age should not bias me around Uma's effectiveness in her new roles. But in this case, I was concerned, maybe because I know her too closely and know about her health challenges. Also, for the last fifty of seventy-seven years, she spent taking care of her husband and family on a full-time basis as her primary responsibility. She never worked professionally in its most commonly used sense of the term during that time or before her marriage either. Can she run the school, manage finances, administration all by herself?

Though I know Uma and the surrounding context fairly well, I was not sure what to expect. Will this end in some kind of crisis where Uma's kids will have to come and close everything down and still have to move Uma to a home after she tried for a few weeks? Or will Uma be so sad and lonely that her health will deteriorate further? I guess the jury is out. Deep in my heart, I wish her success, whatever that means for her.

My tea is finished now. It is also getting late. I have a busy Monday morning with a flight to Denver, which requires me to leave home by four thirty am. This is one of my routine travels for work. Always good to see people in person. I spend a lot of time online, as long as anyone else. I am still to find a better way of connecting with people than in person. Looking forward to a week in Colorado.

I closed the back door, put the cup in the dishwasher, and gave a hug to my wife and son before heading upstairs to get ready for the night.

As I set my alarm for 4 am and try to read the latest book by Robin Sharma, I could not quite focus today. Maybe I should have visited Uma for the funeral, maybe I am overthinking it. Maybe I should plan a visit next year. Maybe her extreme confidence will drive her through the new phase of life, or maybe her confidence will be crushed by realities and her lack of professional skills. Somewhere in there, I dozed off at some point.

Independence

If you are a number nerd like me, you might have calculated Uma's year of birth by now. I am not sure why I do this with dates and numbers whenever I read a book. Funny enough, my eleven-year-old son does that too. Maybe it's genetics.

Once, we were viewing an investment property. As the realtor was showing the property and shared the printout of the listing, my son said, "Daddy, this was built before World War One." Though the house was renovated and was in a relatively good state, I could not get over the visual of two massive world wars passing over it. Everyone who was alive at that time is now dead. We did not end up buying that house for other reasons. I have the exact same habit of connecting memories and stories with major world milestones and calculating years based on stories. I would watch a movie, and if it had some history in it, I would often connect where my dad, my mom, or others were around at that period.

Uma was born in India in July 1947. That is one of the most important milestones for the Indian subcontinent. Uma would often say, "I ended the colonial rule in India. Ha ha, I was so independent and unstoppable that the colonial government had to leave India within one month of my birth."

Uma always enjoyed this coincidence of her birth year with India's independence. Though it is impossible for her to remember, she likes to tell us the story of the first Independence Day celebration in India. Many of them marched barefooted. She spoke of how her parents went to the public gathering to participate in the celebration, with thousands of others wearing Khadi (handmade Indian clothes).

Khadi was a symbol of accepting local over imported. Like our locally sourced organic stores and boutiques we have in North America. The same concept applied to Khadi clothes, which were made from locally grown cotton and woven by locals, as opposed to the imported polyester from England. Khadi was a big symbolic part of Gandhi and his revolutionary journey too. She describes it with a lot of energy and descriptors. Thousands of men, women, and children walked on the streets of Calcutta (now called Kolkata) with a miniature tricolour national flag in their hands. Some adults carried a full-size national flag on their shoulders. No one wore imported clothes. The national anthem and other patriotic songs were playing everywhere. She would add, "It felt like the sun rose that day just for India to express freedom from hundreds of years of colonial government."

I heard this story from Uma several times. It is consistent as if she remembers everything from her one-month age. I asked, "How do you remember all this in so much detail, you were only one month old?" Uma never directly answered the question. She obviously heard the story from her mother, and she heard it so many times, she made it her own. A story she owned and was proud of.

She mentions that their whole household in the north part of Calcutta was decorated with paper chains of tiny national flags. Her dad and all her uncles set up a tall pole to hoist the national flag in front of their house. A feeling my generation will never understand, the ability to celebrate one's national flag without fear or hesitation. We inherited 'freedom' by default. Whether it is Independence Day in India or July first in Canada, it might be a good opportunity to express some gratitude and be thankful to our predecessors who have sacrificed to get us freedom.

I am sure Uma does not remember any of this directly, but it is actually fun to hear every time. She heard the stories over and over from the elders of the family so many times; she loves to live in it.

I recently enjoyed the book called "Nexus" by one of my favourite authors, Yuval Hirari. He talks a lot about storytelling and how the human brain consumes information in the form of stories, and how history demonstrated over and over again that stories drove human actions and reactions over centuries. I love the book. Everything about Uma's stories about Independence Day is a good live example for me.

I observed she always used the words "independence" and "freedom" several times and added a lot of energy to them. She told this story to me, her daughter-in-law, and all the grandkids, which I got to witness. It goes without saying that she told this story several times to her own kids growing up as well.

Uma's parents were born in East Bengal, now called Bangladesh. When political unrest coupled with religious conflicts were growing in that part of the world, Uma's dad and family decided to move to Calcutta. Calcutta, being the major city in eastern India, had relatively more safety and financial potential. They migrated in 1940, rented a house on a large piece of land as most did, worked hard, and tried anything and everything they could put their hands on. It was about survival and living with dignity. Starting from the bottom of Maslow's pyramid, they worked to secure their basic and safety needs while working together as a family. Even then, belonging to the family was critical. Those priorities left little time for building self-esteem and self-actualisation. They were just working to survive.

Political situations kept deteriorating for various reasons. Most people following the Islamic faith felt safer in the eastern part of Bengal, and people following Hinduism preferred to be in the western part of Bengal, where Calcutta is. As a result, more and more friends and family of Uma's dad kept migrating from the east to the west towards Calcutta as they were primarily followers of the Hindu faith.

On a regular basis, more and more friends and family came over from their original villages, with or without notice. There was no text or 'WhatsApp'. There were unreliable and costly long-distance telephone calls or slow and unreliable postal mail. Sometimes the mail letters indicating someone would be coming arrived one month after the family actually showed up.

Very rarely was anyone turned away. Besides being friends or friends of distantly related cousins, they were all connected by the same cause of survival and the human need for dignity.

This process continued for a few years. Then, with India's independence in 1947, East Bengal became part of Pakistan, which was a Muslim-majority country. So, most people following the Hindu religion, like Uma's family, decided to move to West Bengal, the part of Bengal which came under India. Uma's family was in Calcutta, which was already part of West Bengal.

This resulted in more and more visitors and immigrants coming to their house for shelter and to search for a new life. Some stayed for a few weeks, months, or years. Some moved and started on their own shortly after.

At a point in time, there were at least thirty adults and a similar number of children at Uma's house. Everyone who was an adult male other than her dad was, by default, her uncle, and every woman was an aunty. Every boy was like a brother, and every girl was a sister. Uma often refers to this set-up as a 'joint family'. I think it is the size of a small community in a North American context.

Someone needed to be the captain of this ever-growing extended family. Uma's dad was the alpha male in the family, the eldest brother among the young adults, entrepreneurial in nature, and a forward thinker. He was the primary captain of the rented house and the family. It was an important distinction. In some ways, everyone came to Uma's dad's set-up and home for shelter and living.

The East India Company gained administrative rights over portions of India in 1764 and began influencing policy.

Resistance to British rule came in waves, often fierce, such as the Rebellion of 1857. Although the British prevailed long after, the seeds of independence had been sown.

Prior to 1905, the Bengal Presidency was the most populated segment of the British Empire. Leaders had complained that the "British Raj," with over 78 million in population, was too large to administer effectively. However, there was another reason. East Bengal was largely Muslim, while Western Bengal was largely Hindu. This projected "partition" angered the established, English-speaking, unified Bengal leadership. British leaders, committed to their "divide and rule" philosophy, triggered nationalist protests. After several years, the British relented and supported a unified Bengal.

By 1947, the religious tension between Muslims and Hindus escalated to a point where some of the residents began demanding another Partition. By joining with Muslim provinces in the western part of India, Pakistan was established as an independent state. East Bengal became East Pakistan and, in 1971, became Bangladesh.

As the country was going through probably the biggest political change, this region experienced additional turmoil due to the split of the province of Bengal between India and Pakistan.

Even my grandma walked the newly created border with her eight kids in the middle of the night in search of a new life. When I watch movies of countries separating due to political turmoil, families getting separated, my eyes soften. On one of those nights, my dad, as a toddler, walked past the border at midnight with his mom, leaving his dad behind to take care of business and sell properties with the idea of joining them a few weeks later. My dad never saw his dad again. I have never met my granddad. We do not know how he passed away, if he was killed in a communal riot, or if he died of some other cause. I have only seen one photo of him, and that was when I was a child. It was a black-and-white group photo of him standing with some of his brothers. In my dad's case, he and his brothers were the family who came and merged with my dad's uncle's family in Kolkata. There were about a similar number of people in their 'joint family' as well. In this case, my dad's uncle was the head of the super extended joint family. My dad also always referred to his cousins as brothers or sisters, and we referred to their kids the same way.

Like most changes in life those days, change was challenging for Uma's family too. It was a big change for the country and, more importantly, the region. There were a lot of positive emotions around freedom. However, political stability and experience in running a democracy were lacking in the newly formed government. It was like a corporation without any process or governance. Most people were struggling with basic needs like food and shelter. Men were struggling to earn a livelihood, and women to have a family and security.

I have heard many stories and read books from that period in Calcutta. The theme almost always included males struggling to get a respectable livelihood or a job. For females, the goal of life was to get married to a decent man with a job and raise a family. Most males wanted to be employed in a private or public organisation. The public sector was preferred for stability reasons. Since the majority of society was formed based on arranged marriage, the education and employment status of the groom pretty much decided the bride. For the bride, education and cultural skills carried some weight, but looks and family were way more important in the world of arranged marriage. It was a different world. Dads and elder brothers were accountable for finding the right match for their daughter or sister.

In this context, everyone was going through the change. The young adults probably went through the most intensity. Most struggled to get a job. There was just not as much. Like any society during change, some embraced change better than others and were more entrepreneurial.

Uma's dad was the entrepreneurial type. As Uma would often say, "My dad was different than most; he was tall, he was brave, very creative". Uma's dad kept on trying his fortune in different businesses. Back in the day, there was no formal market research or search engine. It was the person, their organic knowledge, and intuition which made or broke a business. I realise that I should have written 'person' instead of 'man'. But I think almost one hundred percent of entrepreneurs in those days in that society were men. Each failure of Uma's dad meant coming close to starvation for the family at large. He kept trying. Partly because he was courageous and partly because he was not academically a scholar with the probability of securing a decent job.

Uma's dad had several failed attempts at various businesses. As his cash was about to dry out, the first one which clicked and started making steady cash was his soap factory. He set up a small factory. With the help of local labour and some of the adults in their extended family, the four-thousand-square-foot factory started making soaps. He had a few salesmen who would load the soap in manual vans or motorised trucks to deliver to the retailers within a fifty-kilometre radius. There was no Walmart or any chain in those days. Neither was there any dominance of Unilever or such multinationals yet. These retailers were all one-off local shops with very low purchasing power. The whole supply chain ran on word of mouth, personal relationships, and trust. Most transactions were cash-based. Credit was in the form of delayed payment tracked in a paper book. People who knew someone in the network often would start to pay a bit later and make sure the balances were noted in a paper notebook.

There was no credit check in the current sense of the term. A credit check was personal references, integrity which was often based on faith. There are always exceptions. Like any sector or society, there are always a few who are always looking to take undue advantage. But in general, the majority of businesses trusted and respected the trust with very little financial regulations or control. Integrity was high, and the value of a verbal agreement was significantly higher.

With the overall economy being so volatile, sometimes creditors failed. It was left up to the creditor and debtor to deal with it. Legal and administrative systems had a much larger problem to sort through.

Uma, meanwhile, started growing up with her own elder brother and several other kids in the family. Uma started going to a girls' school, and her brother went to the boys' school within walking distance of their house. Uma picked up a few extracurricular activities, like singing, dancing, and art, while her brother was a bit less interested in school and kept cruising and playing with other boys in the house and the neighbourhood.

The government at that time was trying to discover itself. It is one thing to lead a revolution from outside the government and another thing to run the administration. Still, there were a lot of nationalistic emotions prevailing, which were often the most dominant focus. Often, fiscal and economic decisions were made based on nationalistic emotions versus economic and financial fundamentals.

As part of one of the changes, the government stopped any further import of engineering machinery of certain categories. Uma's dad took the opportunity. He worked hard to get the licence to be the first manufacturer of plywood-making machines.

Plywood was in high demand and there was a lot of demand for the machinery that manufactured it. The country was literally going through a rebuild. Plywood became an item in demand for the construction of offices, home interiors, and so on. Uma's dad secured a very large section of land near Calcutta airport and started his machinery manufacturing factory. It took off really well in a short time. They started supplying all over India and even abroad. Riches started growing fast.

Uma would often tell stories of how she would sometimes go with her dad to clients' houses during Christmas to exchange gifts. Little Uma sometimes went to the office with him and sat there watching planes take off. Somewhat like my deck in Calgary but much closer and noisier. She always lights up when she talks about her participation in her dad's journey.

From a very early age, she participated in the cultural programmes that were organised in the factory during Foundation Day, National Independence Day and Vishwakarma puja.

Vishwakarma puja is a celebration of the god of workmanship or engineering, which all factories and workers celebrate in that part of the world. Vishvakarma is considered to be the divine architect of the universe. The festival is observed mostly in factories and industrial areas, often on the shop floor. This special day is marked by artists, craftsmen, mechanics, welders, industrial workers, factory workers, engineers, and architects who pray for a better future, safe working conditions, and success in their respective fields. They also pray for the flawless functioning of various machines.

I have memories of Vishwakarma Puja as well. Of course, this is several decades later, in the early '80s. We used to live in a tiny rented apartment in the middle of a community where there were several movie studios. Movie studios were big infrastructure with a huge set-up including fake houses, a fake jungle, a fake farm, and many other constructions. Movies were shot all day there. I have seen several movies in the making from the crowd. In one of the movies, our windows came up in the background when the hero was riding a motorbike with his girlfriend. I watched that movie several times. Weird, hey? Maybe I felt I was part of it through a big stretch of my imagination.

Those studios had a lot of staff who lived within the staff quarters onsite in the facilities. They had kids, families, etc. I was friends with several of them. I went to their Vishwakarma puja and flew kites. This is the day all kids and many adults flew kites. With very congested houses and apartments, there was not enough sky space for flying kites. My kites would often take their last breath in the overhead electric lines which were all over. So, the trick was to gather in the kid's house, which had a terrace higher than those overhead electric lines. I did the same. I went to morning school. By noon, I finished my lunch, school, and was up on a friend's terrace, flying kites. We not only flew kites; we had kite wars in the sky, which is a demonstration of your flying skills and the sharpness of your strings. The sky was full of colourful kites. Some would come close to others, and a war would happen, and one would get cut off from the string. When we got cut off, we tied another to our string and flew until we ran out of kites, string, or the end of the day.

I am sure Uma's brothers and other male kids of the family must have also flown kites. But Uma, being a girl, was more focused on the other aspects of the celebration, such as the musical. As she grew older, she took charge of organising those events too. Uma's dad encouraged her as well. Once, Uma was organising such an event with a set-up stage with other kids and some adults in the factory and there was a power cut. In those often here used to power cuts. Two, three, four hours every day. Factories lost productivity; households used small kerosene lamps. Imagine watching a movie in the theatre and it is stopped in the middle. Business was pretty unpredictable. The phenomenon of power cuts continued for decades. We had kerosene lamps and candles. Uma's dad pointed his cars and trucks towards the stage and provided light from their headlights and let Uma's stage performance complete. Uma still remembers this incident. This was like her dad standing up for her and not letting her fail. Uma has very fond memories from that night.

Over the years, Uma's competencies and love for music and art kept growing. Uma signed up for a singing lesson. She regularly performed at various events at school and at her dad's factory. Someone would have to ask her once, and she happily sang on demand at family gatherings and such. She had zero stage fear and turned into a natural performer.

She also started getting nominated for various competitions. In one of those competitions, she came first and received an award from the hands of the then Governor of West Bengal, Srimati Padmaja Naidu. Uma is so proud of this. This was her moment. She often tells stories of this day, along with the story of the opening ceremony of her dad's factory, where the ministers and bureaucrats came. Uma was present with her dad on both occasions. In the opening event, Uma's idol, her dad, was the hero and in the recital competition, it was Uma herself.

Uma never gets tired of talking about the opening ceremony of her dad's Plywood factory. That was her first conscious exposure to such an event, participated by rich and powerful people of the society. That's when she confirmed the pedestal for her dad forever.

Soon after, in her teens, Uma had a bad tonsil infection. The doctors suggested operating. The doctors suggested not putting more pressure on the vocal cords. I am no doctor, but I know that brought an end to Uma's singing endeavours. She gets sad while talking about this.

That did not stop Uma as she picked up the guitar and started taking lessons. Uma enjoyed her studies and musical endeavours. In the meantime, Uma's parents had a second boy. Uma loved being the elder sister to her little brother.

It was evident among the three kids that Uma was the most curious and inclined towards academics. Her grades were better.

She loved teaching her younger brother and several other default brothers and sisters in the family.

Calcutta was no longer the capital of India. However, Calcutta is considered the cultural capital of India, more so during that period. Calcutta was the epicentre of stage theatres.

The area that hosted most of the stages was not too far from Uma's house. Uma could walk to most of the theatre halls from her house. She fell in love with theatres.

Calcutta theatres are something special. I spent a lot of evenings, like Uma, too, in the '90s. It's an expression of talent I have not witnessed anywhere, including Broadway. The actors were multi-talented. They often wrote their own plays based on some societal issue, local or international. Of course, I watched them thirty years after Uma. By that time, a lot had changed. Everything became a bit more accessible, and I was a young man, unlike Uma.

But back in the '60s, a girl regularly going to theatres was not a very common thing and not very much encouraged. Regardless of any hurdles, Uma hardly ever missed any one of the shows through her teenage, early adulthood. Uma and her friends loved their time in the theatres and the thinking the discussion it often triggered.

Uma also started a small book club with her friends. They will read a book and then discuss and reflect. She also started spending time in the national library checking out books. Just touching and browsing the pages made her happy. Uma says, "Then when I bought a new book, I first smelled it. Haha." Uma says, "I like the smell of a new book more than bright red roses."

Uma loved to spend time in the College Street area. College Street is one of the most interesting locally grown book areas. There were hundreds of bookstores. Some were small, some were fairly large. The oldest bookstore in that area was set up in the late nineteenth century. It is hard not to find any book written in English, Bengali, or Hindi in those bookstores situated along the road over a stretch of less than four hundred metres. Each and every bookstore employee or owner personally knew about most books. Remember, there was no Reddit or Google back in the day. That was Uma's Google. A big part of Uma's pocket money went into buying books.

When she did not like the world around her, she just switched to her imagination mode. She held happiness close to her.

Uma lived in her world of joy and imagination. Always joyful and smiling. At least, that's what everyone saw in Uma. Many years later, I saw the same, always talking and smiling ear to ear. As she would add, "I was the most independent and happy among anyone in my family."

Joint Family

In those days, there were not as many hoardings or advertisements in newspapers, magazines, and television showing a man, a woman, and two children. Such pictures became representations of the ideal lovely-looking family with a car, an apartment building, or whatever the real subject of the advertisement over the last couple of decades. Consumerism of products targeted at the so-called ideal family demographic promoted that visual. Most recently, I have seen a few advertisements with two adults of the same gender as well for certain products. I like the inclusiveness in our modern marketing approach. Growing up, Uma's household did not look anything close to that.

As families living in India, Uma's family participated in what was known as a "Joint Family." This is where several generations lived in the same home, all bound by a common relationship. Each joint family included, for each generation, a husband and wife, their sons, their sons' wives, their children, and unmarried daughters.

My dad had seven living siblings and a few others who did not make it through infancy. Uma's dad had seven siblings too. Seven is no magic number in this case. It was often more than five kids from a couple. The ideal picture for them was to have all siblings and their family living together happily. Interestingly enough, I have not seen any all-inclusive family picture of my dad. I guess there were no mobile cell phones around. Getting a photographer to shoot while everyone was present was not a very likely event. Some families did annual get-togethers and kept memories through family pictures. It is few and far between.

If I asked my dad or Uma's dad, I believe they would not even have agreed with that as a family picture; they would like to include all of their cousins and their families who often lived together. Seven or eight siblings with their parents would be a subset of a household back in the day.

If we define a household as everyone living under one roof, it will be larger and will include multi-generational siblings and their families in some cases.

In families we are familiar with these days, typically, the mom or the dad plays the role of the captain of the household interchangeably.

In such large extended families, someone still needed to play the role of the captain. *That role was usually held by the oldest man, referred to as the head of the family. He made decisions on economic and social matters on behalf of the entire family. His wife typically had control over the household and minor religious practices and often wielded a lot of influence in domestic matters. All income earned from individuals within the joint family was pooled to fund the entire operation, regulated by the head of the family.*

In a typical large extended family, usually the senior-most earning man in the family, usually the eldest dad, is considered the default leader of a joint family. In those days, healthcare was not great. Often, people died early. When that happened, the next in line would be considered responsible for the rest of his siblings and family. It might sound overwhelming and odd in today's context, but there was some extraordinary family bond there. This model was so normal; the word family meant a much larger count than what we think today. That's why, growing up in India, I never used the word cousin. All cousins were like 'brothers' or 'sisters'.

As far as the women in the family are concerned, moms were responsible for the kitchen, cleaning, and household chores. If there was wealth, then there were housemaids who helped. Regardless of the help, moms were accountable for all food and household work. Without contraception being a thing yet, most moms had many kids and fragile health. Typically, a mom did not become the head of the family. The wife of the male leader usually was the de facto leader of all the women members.

Uma's dad was the eldest among the siblings and the most capable from an earning perspective. As a natural rule, he became the captain of the family. Like every other family, all siblings of Uma's dad and their families stayed together as they grew. The sisters were married off, and they typically stayed with their respective in-laws.

There were always lots of activities and people in the house.

Uma had friends from school, music classes, and such. The friends sometimes came over, but they were always outnumbered by the number of siblings always around in the house. Imagine the average number of guests or visitors in that household on any day. Upward of fifty humans had meals every day.

I found that structure very intriguing. By my simple maths, there will be some birthday, anniversary, or something almost every day. It must be fun. Once out of enthusiasm, I said, "That must be fun, something special to do every day."

Uma paused and said, "Some days, my dad took a whole bunch of us in his car for a city tour around the Ganges, and then we spent time at the largest natural park in the city, also known as Maidan. Dad bought us lots of peanuts with shells. We sat around when we came back, put all the peanuts from paper bags made of old newspapers onto a big piece of cloth, and made a circle around it." She added, "There were no plastic bags in those days; all bags for groceries or other merchandise like shirts, pants, and shoes all came in recyclable paper bags or paper-made boxes.

These were usually homemade by local ladies in their homes with old newspapers."

"We were ten to twenty of us on any day in that circle of peanuts," Uma said.

I was going to ask what kind of car your dad owned. Not sure why I did not ask. I guess I remembered that there was no concept of a seat belt back in the day. It's all about how many kids can be fitted in. As a dad of an eleven-year-old, that thought was beyond my safety tolerance in today's context. I guess that's why I did not want to know the answer. But the fun was obviously all-inclusive.

"During festivals, the tailor came to our house and measured all of us. The schedule was known. It used to be on a day when there was no school," Uma continued. "We literally stood in a line. The tailor 'uncle' took our measurements and wrote with a pencil in his tiny notebook. It did not matter if it was a boy or a girl. All kids got clothes made by the same tailor, whether it's a shirt or a dress."

I tried to visualise the story with twenty kids standing in a line and getting measured one by one and all of those getting delivered without error or confusion. A lot more questions came to my mind. How did the boys of similar size identify their shirts after they were washed and dried? I guess it didn't matter as long as they fit.

I asked, "Is it the same fabric for your brother's shirts and your dress?"

Uma was quick. "Yes, we were just too happy to get new clothes that those details did not matter," Uma said. "Blue and pink started much later." I saw a meaningful smile on her face.

She smiled, "Blue, pink and plastic all came later."

I was not sure if I was discussing the past or the future.

I remembered the marketing class in business school and all about categorisation and consumerisation, how we turned the world into pink and blue and are now finding it hard to open up to the spectrum. These days, marketers are after the individualisation of offerings. As we go up Maslow's pyramid, differentiation becomes harder.

Uma's extended family mostly hovered at the base of that pyramid, focused on basic survival. Things that matter to them were more fundamental than most of us experience today.

Once a pattern develops and becomes part of life, it is ingrained in our belief system and it's hard to change. For example, blue is for boys, and pink is for girls. I will not go further into this here. I hope you see that throughout the book.

My wife and I keep our recyclable grocery bags in the car. We actually have a lot of them. Even today, I often forget to take them with us when we enter the grocery store. Then we find ourselves at the till where the cashier asks, "Do you want paper bags or cloth ones?" Almost invariably, I choose the cloth ones as they have a handle and are much easier to carry, potentially being reused many times if we do not forget them in the car. Two decades of free plastic bag convenience have created a habit of walking in empty-handed for groceries and coming out with several plastic bags full of stuff. Old habits are hard to change.

Uma added, "It was fun most of the time; you are never alone."

Uma said, "Then there were so many people, with many priorities and desires."

I smelled 'tea' (or gossip), as my teenage niece would refer to it. I asked, "Tell me more."

Uma said, "It was not always harmonious. My aunts would gossip behind my mom's back sometimes or about another aunt. As my dad was the alpha of the family, there was some jealousy as well."

"I hated those situations and decided early in my life that I would never become the carrier in the gossip trail."

She continued, "Negativity like that distorted my picture of a happy joint family. I tried my best not to participate in adult complexities."

With a smile, Uma added, "Me staying oblivious to family feud made me a safe person for most to confide in." She laughed. "It turned out I knew about most of the gossip."

Sometimes, those negative feelings or stories came up and resulted in conflict in the house. Whenever that happened, I, along with the kids in the house, felt pretty helpless. It involved crying, sometimes some yelling and no talking between conflicted individuals for days or weeks. The kids were under pressure to align with their respective parents, which made it difficult to play.

"I could not deal with the allegations and domestic conflicts; I tried to stay out of it. I was conscious that I was the only daughter of my dad, who was the de facto head of this group called family. I did not want anyone to ever have any chance to complain about me."

She took a pause. "I did not want to impact my dad's stature in the family and outside at any cost. He was my hero." A tiny shine appeared in Uma's eyes. "He was just amazing."

With one hero and many 'brothers' and 'sisters', Uma gracefully traversed through her teens in this extended family.

Acceptance

If Carol Dweck had ranked all the kids, even all the humans of that residence, Uma would have come out on top from a growth mindset perspective. Dweck authored the 2006 book *Mindset*, which details fixed and growth mindsets. The fixed mindset sees a world where your intelligence, talents, and potential are set in stone. Uma was a woman; therefore, her role was set within the limits of societal norms. Her obligations to her joint family were within the home. But Uma had a growth mindset, believing that she could learn and grow, becoming far more than the traditional woman.

When Uma's tonsil problem prevented her from singing in any serious manner, she immediately pivoted to the guitar and kept excelling in the same. When she did not like the reality around her, she went into her imagination mode. She came back and kept

kept chugging along with curiosity and that ever-flashing smile.

Besides human friends, Uma made some unique friends with the characters of her books. In one of his books, Robin Sharma mentioned that everyone needs to have a board to guide them. Some can afford living boards, and others should find them in meaningful books. Uma realised and lived that way decades before I learned the concept in Robin's writing.

Uma read more books than the collective number of books read by the other fifty or so members of the family. Not only in terms of inner growth and personal fulfilment, Uma's quest for knowledge and craft was evident in her academic results.

Uma's hero was her dad, and he was aware of that. However, her dad and everyone else in the family, including her mother and brother, were also more aware that she was born as a girl. Since the role of women was fixed in the culture, violating the expectations came with social consequences. Even though some may have noticed Uma's potential, they couldn't dismiss her gender.

On the day of her birth, it was decided what Uma's profession would be. Homemaker, stay-at-home wife, mom, daughter-in-law, sister-in-law who must be highly skilled in cooking, and other chores around the home. While Uma was enjoying and exploring her world, many around her were busy reminding her of her future goals.

"It was a Sunday afternoon. I had just gotten over missing singing and started falling in love with the guitar," Uma said. "My guitar teacher came for my lesson. I went upstairs to get the notebook. As I was jumping down the stairs with a big smile and lots of energy to start my guitar session for the day, my mom called. 'Umaaa........'" Uma said, "Yes, mom, just heading to the guitar session. Can I see you in 30 minutes?" Uma's mom said, "No, please go and serve the uncles who have sat down for lunch. You need to focus on household work more. You are always focusing on things that do not matter." "There were probably ten other humans in the house like all those 'aunts'; we even had some house help who could have served lunch," Uma added. "But it had to be me." I asked, "why?" Uma said, "so that everyone could see me as an ideal daughter."

Uma faced a wall too high to climb. Obedience was a prevailing cultural value. To violate that role was to disrespect the hierarchy, family unity, and Indian culture. Doing one's duty, accepting moral responsibility, and abiding by societal expectations was important. This was a line any self-respecting woman would not dare to cross back in the day.

Uma did not stand up. Uma went sheepishly to the living area and let her teacher know that she would not be able to do the session today; something urgent came up.

Uma was not happy. But she decided to wear her eternal smile on the way to the dining area before she started serving as per her mom's instruction. Some of the adults in the room said, "Uma is getting better at household work, which is the most essential thing for all teenage girls." "I extended my smile," Uma said, and everyone added a smile to their face in acknowledgement.

As I am writing this section, I cannot avoid thinking about my seventeen-year-old niece. What a lovely, bright girl. Taking the International Baccalaureate (IB) for high school. I am super excited she also started driving this year as she turned sixteen. I will be curious to know her reaction when this book comes out. I love all her reactions to social scenarios. She does not hold back. I wish her freedom of thought forever.

The brothers were busy enjoying their extra freedom as boys, exploring sports, and participating in some business. It was becoming obvious that academics were not their favourites. The business was running very well by then. Honestly, by then, it was doing great despite everything. It was more to maintain, much different compared to when Uma's dad started from nothing.

Uma loved her academics and had a great interest in business. Uma probably spent more time with her dad at the factory, organising social events, visiting clients along with her dad. In the process, she most likely understood the nuances of the business, definitely more than anyone around. Their factory was just beside the airport. Uma sat and read books while watching flights taking off and landing for hours.

Since the history of their business is so interesting, I wanted to learn about it from multiple people in Uma's family when the opportunity presented itself. Everyone else's description I found very transactional. I can tell you with a lot of confidence no one probably had as much clarity as Uma did about their business. They did not have called out printed core values, purpose and customer tagline. But Uma's descriptions cover them all; in addition, Uma's people skills were very strong, and she connected with everyone in the factory and administration of the business. No one other than her dad had as much human connection with the key staff at the factory as she did. All of that was topped by Uma's happy smile. Robin Sharma would have easily called Uma the 'smile master' of the family.

"I do not think anyone even noticed my time and interest in the business was starting to grow," Uma said. "I was just happy around the factory." Everyone counted how many times Uma made the bed for the family, served their lunches, and cleaned the kitchen. As they counted the flying hours to give a pilot licence, someone was counting Uma's household chore hours. Uma was not doing great on those performance indicators as much. Most people around were concerned about how Uma could take off as a bride and wife without those hours.

No one observed that Uma really loved to read books, scoring better marks than anyone in the family, taking the time to practice the guitar, and teaching younger kids in the family.

Everyone noticed that Uma went out every day for college, unlike most other girls in the family. She stayed out for a long time, not spending enough time in the kitchen or gossiping on the terrace with other females in the family.

Uma was breaking the pattern. Uma was too independent. How can that make sense for a girl? That became the important question.

The opinion of all adults in the family of fifty mattered, not just the parents. That's one of the nuances of a 'joint family'. There are too many stakeholders with opinions, often without accountability. One of the friends calls opinions without accountability 'intellectual tourism'.

There is no question joint families gossip a lot. For those with limited economic and educational power, such as a woman in a joint family, gossip provides a way to maintain social cohesion, enforce group norms, and solidify group identity. By talking about one another, scrutinising their behaviours, and projecting intentions, they become the judge and jury toward the offender. Having that unofficial role gives them power, especially the individual who has information that others do not. It also serves as a warning to any other person who is quietly contemplating violating a social norm. Step over that line, and you too, will be subject to the gossip.

In the midst of this, Uma scored high marks in her bachelor's with honours in literature and got accepted to the university for her master's. Uma turned into a lovely-looking young lady with a pleasant personality. Male and female friends started enjoying her company, and Uma enjoyed it as well. Few of her male classmates were working towards becoming a professor after their master's. Uma wanted to be one too. Uma would never share. Maybe Uma dreamt of a life with her and one of her friends as a future husband. Both teaching at a college, reading lots of books, watching theatres as soon as the first show, and living a life of growth every day to embody Carol Dweck's ideal growth mindset character.

As Uma started excelling in her academics, art, and social likeability, it became a more serious concern for most in the family. Now, Uma's dad felt the need to act fast to find her a suitable groom and get her married.

Settling the daughter with a decent groom was considered a key responsibility of the dad and elder brother in the family. The typical process was to solicit and/or respond to similar families soliciting a marriage proposal. Often, relatives brought forward proposals. Due to the lack of Tinder or other matchmaking sites in those days, human matchmakers existed as a profession too. Sometimes, they were engaged for a small fee.

Maybe there was a special friend who was part of the story. Uma always starts talking about this phase with a lot of energy and then somehow she holds back and abruptly says, "In those days, decent girls married with the groom arranged by their parents. Parents whose daughter made their own decisions were not considered respectable, and the community often looked down on the parents. It was different."

I asked, "Your dad seems to be a huge supporter of you and a progressively successful man."

"He definitely was."

I asked, "Why did you not ask him to let your life be the way you want?"

Uma paused. She did not quite answer that question.

Uma knew better. Uma was not going to see her hero being looked down. So, the self-selection of the groom was out of the question. Arranged marriage was the norm at that time and often exceptions landed in difficult situations like unacceptability with families and society.

But Uma was scared to leave her reading, her university, theatres and be like her mom. She knew that was exactly the life waiting for her if she married someone like their family, a well-off business house.

Uma knew she could only pick so many battles. She cannot get it all. She was born a girl and her life could not continue like that forever.

Uma's parents and elder brother became active in organising her marriage and started looking for a match through a traditional arranged marriage. Uma knew she might get away with letting them know her preferences, but asking to marry someone of her choice would be out of bounds.

Uma's dad was doing very well financially at that time. Uma checked off a lot of other boxes for an attractive bride. Lots of proposals came from similar families. I asked, "What do you mean by similar families?"

She said, "They were cash-rich and education-poor."

Uma added, "I started getting uncomfortable as I dressed up and sat in front of potential groom and in-laws for interviews over and over again." It was mostly rejection from Uma's family. In the process, Uma accumulated some courage to put forward some preferences. Uma says, "One thing I told my mom is that I will only marry an educated person." Uma chose education over wealth.

It is also not common for a bride to establish her choice. But Uma was not the norm. She spoke up and made her choice known.

Uma believed education would create a future of hope, a future of liberty, a future of rights to make her own decisions.

Although Uma could not stand up for what she really wanted, she did stand up for her preference for knowledge.

With the hope of some independence and the hope of completing her master's, Uma agreed to finally marry an engineer and the son of a professor at the Science College.

Among everything, Uma saw the light of hope to protect parts of her dream: her books, guitar, and her university studies. She knew she would lose her friends, but she hoped to be best friends with her husband and make him her partner for her personal book club and a theatre buddy.

Stakeholders were all aligned and felt reasonably good. Uma got to stand out as the only female in the family with a groom with a formal college degree and hang on to some of her dreams. Uma's dad and brothers felt like achieving the milestone of getting Uma married before it was considered too late. I'm not sure if Uma's mother participated in the decision. But I am sure she must have felt good to find her only daughter complying with the norms.

Restart

Uma's dad was her hero. I know I have mentioned this several times already. Trust me, if you talked to Uma about her childhood, she says that more than once a minute. She always wanted everyone to like and respect him at all times.

Just after the independence of India, most families struggled with basic needs, suffering from unemployment, often hoping the male member of the family would secure a government job. Unfortunately, those jobs were almost non-existent. Uma's dad decided to be an entrepreneur. He would become an employer by taking care of the large extended joint family. This created employment directly and indirectly. While everyone was expecting the economy to take care of them, Uma's dad started contributing to the Global Domestic Product (GDP).

Uma used to get 'pocket money' for personal miscellaneous expenses. Uma's pocket money was more than the typical family income of an eight-person family in India at that time. Uma was blessed to be in abundance all her time with her parents. Uma often bought ice cream or other snacks for her friends while taking a long walk from university back home.

Uma sometimes helped people in need around the house, like house help, their kids, and others with very low income, without any sort of insurance or financial stability. This is a trait I have seen Uma carrying with her even now.

Interestingly, poverty was a very common thing with Uma's classmates in school and college. Literally everywhere. Most people struggled to make ends meet. There were thousands of homeless people on the streets of Kolkata. Despite that prevalent scene of scarcity, Uma was unfamiliar with the experience of poverty.

Uma dreamed of being like her dad, breaking the pattern, having a meaningful purpose, and doing whatever she thought was meaningful.

Everyone in the family and friends, however, looked for similarities between

Uma's dad and her two brothers, though there were not too many. To be fair, the context was different. Uma's dad was a visionary and a builder. Uma's brothers grew up in abundance with the intention of inheriting and maintaining. On the other hand, Uma was different. She had a natural leadership, helping others, going to university, theatres more and more, and started to be seen as the outlier in not a positive way.

What all eyes in the family were now looking for in Uma were her household skills of cooking, serving food, cleaning dishes, and so on. No one was looking for her dad in her; everybody was busy comparing her with her mom.

Uma's dream and expectations were tested once she married. Meanwhile, the well-wishers hoped that Uma would change her priorities and become a great homemaker like her mom. They were hoping that after she married, she would take care of her husband and in-laws, cooking, cleaning, and making everyone happy. They anticipated a raving report card from the in-laws.

At the same time, there were others waiting for Uma to fail. In their jealousy, they reasoned that if Uma failed in her domestic duties, it meant her family failed. Most importantly, the captain, her father, would fail. Uma, feeling the family pressure, was nervous for the first time in her life. On one hand, the Carol Dweck girl was ready to pivot, becoming the best friend of her engineer husband, hoping to even start a personal book club where they both read books and had conversations. After work and her university, Uma wished they went to theatres without anyone putting a timeline for returning home. There were no restrictions now that she was with her husband.

"At the same time, I was not sure," Uma says. "Besides the husband, there were three sisters, two brothers, and my in-laws in the same house." Uma is familiar with the joint family, but she heard through the family gossip trail that her husband's house is much smaller and not in great condition. Someone even told her that they were very poor. Uma has seen the poor in the streets and theatres, but not up close.

Going through all these fears, Uma maintained her wide smile. Uma knew one thing: she did not want to repeat her mom's life.

Uma followed tradition and came to her husband's house after the marriage. She focused on the positive, knowing that unlike anyone else in her family, her husband was an educated engineer and his dad a professor. Uma knew the house was very small, so she adjusted her imagination. Instead of a house with lots of books, there would be a bedroom with a wall-to-wall bookshelf overflowing with books. She also imagined the rooms were filled with light gramophone music in the evening.

Reality, however, shocked Uma when she walked in. There was not a single book or magazine to be seen in this whole three-bedroom house. Floors were wet, walls had damp patches, and paint was overdue. They showed Uma her room. It was a nine-by-eight-foot space with a double bed filling most of it. The room was right adjacent to her in-laws' room on one side and her three sisters-in-law and two brothers-in-law on the other.

Her father-in-law, the professor, continued the guided tour. After a one-minute stop at her bedroom and walk-by of the other two rooms, they arrived at the kitchen. "Now, this is the most important room in the house," Her first impression made her sick. Had there been a bathroom nearby, Uma would have thrown up in disgust. The kitchen featured a large charcoal wood fire pit for a stove, several buckets of water, and a very yellow, low-power light bulb. The walls were caked in charred marks from burning coal, dry wood, and cow dung cakes. Uma cringed in fear at the thought of working in that environment for hours on end.

Uma, lost in her thoughts, came back to reality with the sound of giggles. Others had arrived to see the newlywed bride. Instead, she wanted to run to the bathroom and hide. Unfortunately, no one had shown her the bathroom yet. She later learned the bathroom was thirty feet from the main house. There was a hand pump well and a municipality water tap between the house and the bathroom.

Despite the disappointing condition of the home and the horrible vision of her future, Uma put on a happy face. On the outside, she was smiling and bubbly as always, but on the inside, she was ready to run back to her dad's house as fast as she could. There she could hide behind a big pile of books, or maybe hide in the backstage of a theatre hall. She imagined running back towards her dad, but there were many stakeholder faces between her and her hero. Then, to make the vision even worse, she imagined her hero saying to her, "I knew she would be a failure after all."

She knew she could not run away without bringing shame to her dad. To violate this traditional pattern, she would impact her hero's image for everyone. She pivoted quickly to find a way to make it work. The Carol Dweck growth mindset girl reappeared. Despite a determination to make this work, Uma wondered how her dad could agree to marry her off to this house. "Why did he choose this house when he knew my desires? How could he think this is a liveable condition for me? Did he even know how bad it was?" That lifted her chin, thinking, "Maybe he did not. It was possible in those days that someone else might have come for a visit, not her dad himself." As comforting as that thought was, none of that mattered anymore. This was her new home. Nothing was going to change that.

Since most women were married before the age of twenty at that time, there must have been pressure on her father. By this time, Uma was much older, and the family must have felt worried. At least, that's how Uma reconciled it.

She has not been easy with setting those key performance indicators (KPIs). For Uma, she desired a graduate groom. Technically, I guess her dad and elder brother delivered to her KPI. However, they didn't go beyond the metric. Yes, he checked that box but didn't foster the reason why that metric was set. She loved learning and wanted a family where learning was a priority. For her to have one without the other was not a win.

I can't stop thinking this is exactly what happens to KPIs without context in the corporate world. Numbers are met and intent gets lost along the way. Is there any wonder that companies struggle and fail in the same way Uma did in her new joint family?

Even today, corporate America struggles with KPIs without context. Corporations just did the same with Equity, Diversity and Inclusion (ED&I). Instead of investing in a culture of psychological safety and inclusion for all, including the majority, most organisations created quarterly targets based on KPIs: the number of females at various levels, including boards, the number of people of colour, those with disabilities, and so on. Patterns of hundreds of years cannot be broken fast with KPIs. Now, in the media, there are several examples of large organisations letting go of their ED&I teams. I predicted this outcome several years back in my book 'Let's Do It Right'.

Those seats-of-the-pants, fast-paced initiatives have left behind a bad taste of exclusion with a lot of people who represent the majority in a community. As a result, bad incidents happen, and the entropy of hate increases in our society.

A few months back, my professor at Columbia University, NY, was walking to the university on a Saturday morning when two bikers decided to stop, slap, abuse him, and call him names because of his colour. This incident makes me sad but even angrier. I am angry about the system, the quarter-based approach to solving bigger social issues, which leaves a large population with a feeling of exclusion. This is exactly what urged me to write 'Let's do it right'. My professor was a victim, and so was the offender. As they say, behind every anger, there is fear. Those short-term policies and KPIs have scared the majority of the population and done no good to anyone.

Sorry, I had to make the point before continuing with our Uma. I am just saying Uma and her family checked the box for Uma's desired metric, and now here she is in utter poverty. Though her husband and father-in-law were graduates and educated in the traditional sense, there was no love for education, only some degrees for livelihood. They had zero appreciation for Uma's academics or passion for arts.

That left Uma with very few choices, maybe none. Being from a richer family, she could have taken the route of complaining and gone back to her dad and then worked out something. There was another option: adopt Carol Dweck's model mindset and turn the ship around. However, this was a big ship. However smart and well-read Uma was, this was a different domain. Uma realised this was definitely a reboot of her life.

Decades back, when my wife and I moved to the West, we found ourselves in a one-room suite in not at all fancy apartments. We had to factor in slow elevator time during busy hours. Sometimes, the wait for elevators could be about ten minutes. There was no dishwasher. We used the common laundry room, which did not feel comfortable at all. We always took the transit as we did not yet have a driver's licence and car even at minus forty. Once, we tried to walk five blocks with groceries on a Sunday evening at minus thirty-five. Those five blocks felt like five miles.

Just a week before the move, my driver back in India would not even let me carry my laptop bag to the car and back. Large house, all paid for, supported by two house helps. We can't even remember when we went to the kitchen and cooked something for us. Maybe an instant noodle once a year or made coffee once a month. Most importantly, lots of family and friends around.

It was a change. A big one. I know a lot of immigrants who moved like us in the early or middle of their careers. We all handle it differently. Some isolate themselves and hang out with people of similar backgrounds, countries, or origins. Others just adopt and embrace. We also had two choices. One, work hard, save money, hang out with people who look like us, have similar regions of origin, or be part of the society we chose as home, integrate, build relations, and adopt the change. We decided to take the latter route and absolutely integrated into the ecosystem with the greatest friends ever. Immigration is not easy. It's a restart. We are so glad we did. And we offer our sincere gratitude to the friends and colleagues who made us part of their lives.

For Uma, the change of scene was no less material than us moving thousands of miles across the oceans and adopting a completely different country as home. Though the distance between Uma's in-laws' house and her dad's home was barely ten kilometres, the change was no less than ours.

Uma decided to integrate and change from within the new set-up. And she did restart and started learning to fit in and focus on the skills she always avoided and be that ideal wife, and daughter-in-law.

Struggles And Stubbornness

Eleven adults, three rooms, one bathroom and, of course, the kitchen. Here starts Uma's married life. Since her husband was the elder and only married son, she was lucky to get a room with a door.

Uma liked two types of books: sociopolitical and romantic novels. They shaped Uma's thinking over the years. Her married life was not really romantic at that time. Within the room, she fulfilled her duty as a wife, and outside, she kept trying to satisfy the ever-changing job description of a daughter-in-law. No one cared about the sociopolitical viewpoint of a newlywed young lady. All theatre and books which talked about utter poverty and constant family feuds were now alive for Uma.

Daily conflict between family members and loud yelling was normal. Besides Uma's husband and father-in-law, there was very limited literacy in the whole family. Being literate, educated, and loving learning created jealousy and a hostile environment. Uma faced resistance to literally every opinion she expressed.

To ensure social stability and help Uma understand the role she was to play, Uma's new family had a report card system. Every day, she was graded on how well she performed her duties. Uma's in-laws would release a virtual report card every day in the evening for her husband after he returned from work. Imagine how she must have felt. Every day, she was observed, scrutinised, and then held accountable to her husband for what she had done when he was at work. Here was an educated woman subjected to undesired duties and then judged. Daily performance appraisal on tasks she did not enjoy doing at all. Uma spent all day performing chores she did not enjoy and then got a poor evaluation at the end of the day. Uma was embarrassed, felt violated, and a bit angry.

Imagine that at work, you have a performance evaluation every day, and you are working on everything you do not want to work on. That was exactly Uma's situation.

Meanwhile, despite not-so-great feedback, Uma got promoted to the role of chef and head of cleaning and hospitality in the house. This time, there was no resistance from anyone. This means Uma was given responsibility for all cooking and cleaning for the household. Remember, Uma is a woman and a housewife. Isn't she supposed to have been perfect at all through her growing-up years?

Remember, I said that Uma was a model character for Dweck's growth mindset. She wasn't about to quit. Instead, she was determined to excel.

Uma started waking up at four in the morning every day so that she could prepare food for everyone and do as much as she could, including providing breakfast for her husband before he went to work. She was hoping that by completing more work before leaving home, there would be fewer complaints from her in-laws.

She wasn't going to give up and set aside her love of learning for cooking and cleaning. Instead, as the social pioneer she is, she set out to prove she could do both.

Uma continued her university studies. That was the best part of her day. A break from the grind. But it did not continue for too long. Her performance appraisal at the end of the day started deteriorating rapidly, and no one else supported her continuing university after marriage. Her folks first started scrutinising her schedule. Then, very soon, Uma was on a performance improvement plan.

Uma gave in once again and quit university halfway through. The only support she had was her books; all living beings around her found the university an unnecessary waste of time.

Uma looked around. "I'm not sure who I was hoping would stand up for me," Uma said. "I myself did not."

After that, Uma became just another woman, a wife. Cook, clean, serve, cook and again and again, just like her mom.

One thing that distinguished Uma from others in her in-laws' house was her access to cash. Uma still kept getting her 'pocket money' from her dad's house. All of it was going into filling up the financial gaps in her in-laws' family. Uma's husband did not earn much. There was a perennial financial gap. Uma regularly kept selling her gold ornaments for cash in addition to her pocket money.

A new thing was added to her daily performance feedback. Whenever there was a need for money, there was an implicit expectation that Uma would get it from her rich parents. Since Uma came from a much richer family, it was expected that Uma would bring lots of financial support with her. It was not uncommon back in the day for the bride's dad to financially help the groom and the family. Instead of going to her parents, she kept selling her ornaments so that the ship would keep sailing.

Uma said, "I kept smiling and listening to all the abuses. I kept smiling in front of my hero so that he does not feel bad. I kept looking happy with my in-laws so that my marriage kept going. I decided long back that I must always be happy and smiling to the world; what happens in my mind is mine."

"I decided not to join or start any victim fest," Uma said. "Maybe I was trying to be positive, or I knew there was not any place for me to share without being judged."

Uma started living her mom's life just in a very poor and rough way. Meanwhile, Uma's first son was born. It was a boy, so everyone was happy, even Uma's mother and father-in-law.

Uma shifted her thinking towards her son and how to turn around the environment for her son. This provided a new purpose for Uma. A chance to revive her dreams and allow her son to live them. Once again, that smiling girl, now a woman and mom, pivoted her focus. Uma's dreams paused in favour of her son.

Stood Up

She was redefining her purpose and strategy, which was now focused heavily on her husband and her son. "How could I break the pattern of perennial poverty, yelling, and disrespect?" Uma said, "That was top of my mind."

Uma knew that her husband needed to earn more. Significantly more to break out of this loop. His job would never get him there.

Uma encouraged him to get out of the job and start something on his own. After several months of hesitation, finally, her husband started his business. He started a construction company. As expected, Uma sold more jewellery and borrowed more money from her extended parental family to get the business going. Several years of losses and struggle continued. Maybe about a decade. Uma kept selling her jewellery, getting loans from her richer relatives. But it was never enough. They made roads, public facilities like parks, memorials at that time. With Uma's connections, financial support and patience, the business finally started rolling.

Uma never told me whether she was the brains behind the business strategy and plan.

I think she was. She was the only one with business acumen and a bit of observed experience. I believe that she undersells her contribution. It was way beyond financial.

The bedroom turned into a workplace after six thirty in the morning, seven days a week. There were no other space options. Her husband, with his newly appointed employees, met in the morning to plan their day. After a cup of tea from Uma, they all went with their teams to construction sites.

Uma's husband worked seven days a week, month after month and year after year. "In those days, we did not go for a vacation or something grand; we did some local days here and there between projects," Uma said.

Uma's son either slept with them or with his grandparents. As Uma's son became older and school started, Uma decided to create an environment for him so that he could become that 'educated' person surrounded by books. He was modelling Uma.

By then, all of Uma's sisters-in-law had married and moved to different places or households. The brothers-in-law both moved out. Uma sold several of her jewellery pieces and took secret loans from relatives on her parents' side to fulfil the so-called responsibilities of Uma's husband towards his siblings, as assigned by his dad.

The third bedroom in the house became available, and Uma wanted it to be designated to her son. She envisioned tables and bookshelves around it. Uma proposed, and her father-in-law disposed. "That room needs to be available for all other kids and their families to come and visit us. It cannot be allocated to Uma's son."

Uma already accepted she is a 'woman'. Her primary job is as a cook and cleaner at home. This time, she did not. The mom was stronger than the wife.

After many years of work finally, Uma's husband was less financially reliant on Uma's sources for his business. He stood beside Uma, and they decided to move to a larger house nearby.

Though Uma was good at her studies, she always missed the fact that she was not taught in English, which was rapidly becoming India's working language. Uma again stood up and decided that her son would be going to an English-medium Catholic school. The school was one hour away from their place. The local public school would have been a free and popular suggestion.

But you can imagine that decision was yet another violation of her joint family's expectations. There was enough criticism from her in-laws on her decision. They were worried about the lost service hours from Uma as she focused on travelling to school every day.

This became a "line in the sand" where Uma would stand her ground. She had given up her dreams of living a learned life; she would not sacrifice her son's potential. So Uma set her mind, stood her ground, and was ready with a plan.

She started waking up earlier than four in the morning, did her expected chores so that she could take her son to school every day.

Uma's husband's construction business started taking off, and with Uma's influence, he started looking at the bigger world. He started accompanying Uma to theatres over low-quality movies. He bought a car for the family and started taking family vacations.

Despite her obedience during their early married years, Uma was still Carol Dweck's poster girl for a growth mindset. She decided to live and grow as a family. She refused to sacrifice her life and her family's potential by bowing down to the fixed mindset.

In the summer of 1980, with the Olympics coming up, she saw a great opportunity. The local government decided to gather and support a group of delegates. The deal was that you had to pay your own costs, and any selected family would be supported with a visa to visit Russia and another country while on the tour. Uma had her husband stand in the line from midnight to make it to the list. Central to that growth mindset is the willingness to exert whatever effort is necessary to secure the opportunity. Uma not only loved to read and dream of doing great things, but she was also a woman of action. She would keep her eyes and ears open for opportunities, then prepare diligently to have the best chance of success. They did get selected. Uma and her husband were preparing to be the first couple from Uma's in-laws' family to ever visit a foreign country.

It feels weird to write about Russia and the USA in one sentence other than the context of conflict in today's context. It is hard to envision the Olympics being held in Russia. World geography, economics, and politics have shaped it over the years, fascinating me.

Uma had an uncle who was much younger than her dad. He was one of the best and brightest in academics in their extended family. In the late seventies, he moved to the USA and joined NASA as a junior engineer. Uma was curious, knowing that NASA triggers interest and curiosity in most, particularly in people from the eastern part of the world. Uma wanted to come and visit. This is Uma's way of exploring the 'universe'.

Uma and her husband left their son with her in-laws and also received some support from her mom. Uma and her husband decided to go watch the Olympics and then visit the NASA uncle.

Uma was a free spirit, challenging the social expectations from the beginning.

She had not performed her duties well as per her in-laws, especially in the early days of the marriage. Then, she had the audacity to send her son to an English-speaking school. But the criticism reached its peak when she wanted to travel to the United States. Imagine their horror, a mom leaving her son behind for her own desires. Of all the ways she had tried to violate their standards, this was the worst. It was bad, bad, bad. They were convinced that spending so much money on something which is not necessary was beyond any level of acceptance. It was very, very bad.

But Uma was determined this time and stood strong.

Uma and her husband left for the one-month tour. They visited Russia, watched the Olympics and then went to the United States. If you ask Uma about all the vacations in her life, she will spend eighty percent of the time talking about this trip. This trip checked a lot of boxes for her.

This vacation was a turning point for Uma. Not only was it exciting and enjoyable, but having taken this adventure, it changed her standing in the family and community.

By visiting that foreign land, she was showing her family that she was no longer poor, which made her feel elite like her dad with ministers during their factory opening. She says, "There were lots of ministers travelling with us as part of the delegation."

In the US, they travelled in Greyhound buses from one coast to the other. She used to talk about Greyhound. Later, when her kids moved to North America, Uma realised that Greyhound was not a good status symbol for transportation. So, she started skipping that part shortly after.

I have known Uma for about twenty years. I have heard at least a hundred times that her uncle at NASA used to play tennis every day. Sometimes, she called while I was just entering my tennis game, mentioning the uncle's story to the point I was getting late for my game. But it is not annoying; it is sweet. This is how she learned every day and defined and refined what her good looks like for her and her family.

Since it was very hard for her as a woman to follow her dreams, she started living through her husband and son. Guess what sport Uma signed up her son for after coming from the trip?

Tennis. That added to her already busy drive to and from school every day. Soon after coming back from the tour, Uma had her second child. Her daughter was born and would soon become a mini-Uma.

Thirty-plus years had passed since Uma was a kid. She hoped society had outgrown many of its fixed mindset ways, but she was disappointed when so many were quick to criticise the complexion of the girl child when she was born. Remember, she will have to be married off one day and fairer is better. This baby child was simply too dark-skinned, so the gossip mill ground out the negative projections. Little did they know the power of Uma and her new baby.

They also continued with the criticism of Uma's intent to send her daughter to that same Catholic English-medium school. What's the point of driving that far every day? Why not send her to the free girls' school in the community?

They couldn't see beyond their limitations. Why does the girl need to learn other things like singing, recitation, dancing? Why give her English books like Tintin or Nancy Drew? Her in-laws, like the rest of the joint family, had strong opinions, none of which agreed with her dream.

But again, Uma had sacrificed her life; she wasn't about to sacrifice her daughter's. Uma stood up. Her daughter went to the Catholic school as well. The girl went for dance, singing, and recitation lessons that the best Uma could arrange and took her everywhere around. The good thing was they could afford a car for Uma now, which made Uma's life easier to drive around the two kids to activities, school, and other places. Uma spent upwards of five hours in the car on average every day. There was a driver who knew every backroad of the three-hundred-year-old city of Calcutta. The time in the car with the kids, shopping for the family, and visiting her dad's house became a happy place for Uma.

Over the weekends, Uma started going to the theatre with her husband. Uma's husband, with encouragement from Uma, started climbing Maslow's pyramid. He began to see more than simply providing the basics. He too, was developing a growth mindset.

During this time, Carol's girl kept chugging along upward and forward, which pleased her immensely.

Acceptance Again

Uma's daughter is a replica of her, just a newer version. I know her well, and rejecting the status quo is a core part of her approach to life. Growing up, she read more books than anybody I knew. Through those books, she learned about the cultures of various countries, types of civilisations, and other fascinating topics. She turned out to be a curious and extroverted soul.

Even today, she absorbs all sorts of knowledge very quickly. When people ask her about something, let's say about a restaurant, she not only provides feedback on the food but also the story behind the place, when it was started, who the owner is, and their passion for the menu. Those who know her well prefer asking her about things rather than 'Google' or 'ChatGPT'.

Mark is a close friend of Uma's daughter's husband. Mark got his friend a T-shirt with the caption, 'I have my wife; I do not Google.'

She is a brave spirit. She is extremely intelligent as well. She was outstanding in academics. She continued singing, recitation, and dancing without really loving any of those aspects.

That's not to say she is perfect. At times, she pushes back on the status quo a bit too much. As intelligent as she is, as a child, she did silly things, like planting car keys, expecting to see a car grow. She's human, but an impressive one. Nothing seems to be beyond her grasp. She wanted to be included in the mainstream action of the house, rather than relegated to the traditional woman's role. She wanted to play tennis and swim like her brother. She even wanted to be at the construction site, see the concrete work, and learn the business.

But the only decision-making she ever got involved with was their annual vacations. Her brother outsourced the work to her, so she was in charge of the place, dates, and other logistics. She gladly accepted the challenge and executed it well. This became a task that she took pride in and became an annual project she could do together with her brother.

Uma was pleased that she secured most of the things her daughter needed to make her an independent person. She got her the Nancy Drew and Tintin books as well as hundreds of other books, which little Uma enjoyed. Uma also made sure she read books on mythology and the classics. Uma beamed with pride when her daughter had the room Uma dreamed of with wall-to-wall, ceiling-to-floor bookshelves. Less than three percent of the space was filled with dolls and toys. One of Uma's biggest accomplishments was accompanying her son and daughter to school every day, attending adjacent Catholic schools. Uma's daughter also enjoyed going with her mother to visit the open fish market, and regularly visiting Uma's brother and family on the way. They both enjoyed the proximity of family.

Both of Uma's kids have fond memories of stopping for ice cream on the way back from school. Uma's son loves sweets, while her daughter loves a variety of good food.

Uma's husband, however, has a more traditional view of his daughter. He wanted her to continue excelling in academics and be ready for the world in a way he thought successful girls should. This involved both academics and activities, such as dance, to then attend an Ivy League university for higher studies. Ultimately, his goal was for her to be desirable marriage material. He clung to the old practice that unmarried daughters were nothing more than temporary residents. Though he supported and encouraged her in many ways, he struggled to adopt his wife's and daughter's dreams. He worried that the challenge-everything attitude of his daughter would conflict with her desirability as a bride.

While I disagree with his vision, I do not blame Uma's husband at all. He was a victim of the pattern he was raised with and lived under his entire life. He could not get beyond his definition of a successful girl, even seeing his accomplished daughter.

While Uma's daughter was growing and becoming independent, so was the business. The business succeeded to such an extent that the family was flush with cash and the factory needed to be expanded. Unfortunately, Uma's dad passed away, gradually diminishing the funds received from her parents.

With the business profits, they expanded the six-storey home. The latest renovation saw the installation of a much-needed elevator and a new marble nameplate. Unfortunately, the nameplate proudly displayed everyone's name except Uma's daughter. Just as temporary residents usually do not have passports, so too, their names were not included on the home's nameplate.

I asked Uma why she did not stand up. How could she allow her daughter to receive the same treatment Uma resisted all her life?

Uma first tried to justify the decision. Then she realised that did not make a lot of sense. Finally, she defeatedly said, "That was as much as I could stand up for. I had to accept the rest."

Even now, after so many years of pushing the boundaries, Uma knows that a person can only push so far.

A few years back, Uma's daughter, who now lives in the West with her husband and two-and-a-half-year-old son, visited Uma's house. It was her son's first visit to India. He worked very hard with his limited vocabulary to read the letters on the nameplate. He had already heard many stories about his mommy's childhood in this mansion with six floors, twenty-three bathrooms, an elevator, and a dedicated security guard. He carefully read all that was written on the nameplate. To his dismay, he could not find his mom's name. He asked, "There is a problem. Mommy's name is not there. How is this mommy's house? Her name is missing."

The questions from young children exposing our tolerance of old patterns make for uncomfortable moments for parents. We try to answer even though we know our failure is exposed. It's funny because when these same kids grow up, they find themselves in the same situations with their children.

Reality is the pattern. The traditional pattern for unmarried women in India prevailed, and Uma accepted it. My wife and I have three bedrooms in our house. One is for my son, one is our master bedroom, and the other we call my niece's room. We consider her like a daughter who deserves a dedicated room. While she has her own room in her house, she has a special place in our life.

Another part of the pattern puzzled me. One day I asked Uma why she never considered her daughter in the decision to run and grow their primary construction business. Uma said, "The sector is very bad and not suitable for girls. Instead, we wanted her to be highly educated, a professor, or something."

I wondered, "How is that different from Uma's family wanting her to be a homemaker?"

Fortunately, that pattern has faded in the last thirty years. But still, girls must think and act in a certain way. They must not stray too far from that invisible line of obedience.

Because I know Uma's daughter so well, I can confidently say she would have taken the business to new heights. She is that type of leader. Like her mother, she has a Carol Dweck growth mindset.

I also know Uma's son fairly well. He is one of the most amazing people I know. He is extremely talented and professional, a great dad and husband.

It still bothers me that we do not ask girls what they really want to do. We default the boy to something he may or may not want to be. As a society, we not only create patterns for girls but also for boys as a result.

I am not sure if this is a boy and girl discrimination or if it is just hard to evolve and break patterns.

I think it is the patterns. Patterns are those social practices that repeat throughout the culture and from generation to generation. The patterns detail what is acceptable and what is not. Patterns establish the beliefs, values, and behaviours of the culture, setting the stage for proper interaction and expectations. They serve as boundaries, sending signals warning members of the danger zone for violations. Patterns also give licence to gossip about those skirting the grey areas, punishing those who dare to consider alterations. It is best never to break the pattern, or even approach a grey area in a black and white pattern. In their repetition, patterns become ingrained, fostering further repetition. Patterns have their own way of protecting themselves against change.

The patterns also set the boundaries of acceptable behaviour. Patterns condone the exclusion of those unwilling to accept the pattern. Supporters of the pattern assume that the pattern is correct, justified, and productive, even if an objective observer disagrees.

Challenging patterns is difficult because their existence is difficult to define. When asked why one follows the pattern, you may hear a variety of answers. First, "That is the way we have always done it." Next, you might hear, "It's natural. That's the way it works best." Third, some would explain, "It was designed by the gods," making any logical argument void. How do you argue with someone who believes an all-powerful deity established the pattern? To challenge the pattern is heresy, tempting the fierce anger of the unseen. It is tempting fate by incurring the wrath of the universe, or at least, the faithful.

Uma challenged the patterns. Small changes were tolerated (but not encouraged), but anything beyond minor changes received harsh reactions. She knew she had pushed the boundaries as far as she could without destroying any potential success within the system.

We have our patterns today. When you get into an emergency and a nurse comes in, you expect the nurse to be female. When you call a plumber for a leak at home, we expect a guy to show up in his truck. But notice that acknowledging those patterns is healthy. The patterns are ingrained if we discourage men from becoming nurses or women from becoming plumbers.

Patterns are not all bad. Actually, patterns are very valuable until they hold back progress.

I remember several years ago, a few of my board colleagues and I had the opportunity to talk with a teenage boy who was supported by welfare. After listening to him and what he was doing, we asked what was the most important thing missing in his life. We expected to get an answer along the lines of poverty or some financial scarcity. Instead, he said, "I am missing a male role model in my life."

We struggled with his response and asked, "How come?"

He said, "Almost all of the teachers in my school are female. I am the oldest child in the family and my dad is either working one of his three jobs or drunk and sleeping."

None of us would have ever guessed that. Evidently, another pattern blinded me from seeing the solution to his problems.

This young man was saying that to grow into a successful, good adult male, he needed a good pattern to follow. Instead, all he had was a broken pattern leading to failure.

He was wise in recognising the value of a good pattern.

Meanwhile, I recognise that Uma's daughter's context was thirty years later than Uma's time. Uma and her husband tried to give her the best life possible within the limits defined by what they knew. Uma's daughter also did not get to make her choices until she became an adult. Despite the thirty-year difference, the pattern persisted.

Landing

My thoughts got interrupted. Not necessarily a bad thing. I was getting judgemental. The pilot, following the patterns established for safe air travel, just announced that we were starting our descent to the Denver airport. That signalled to me that I was about to implement the next stage of my travel pattern. It was going to be a busy day where I went from the airport to the Avis red bus, picked up my rental and then went to my destination. That pattern, i.e., routine, worked well for me.

I recognise there is value in patterns and habits. They often take away surprises and bring predictability. I like my habits and patterns as they help me comfortably navigate through the journey called life. However, the context and variables around the patterns keep evolving. When they change enough, then patterns, like a societal 'ego', try to hang on to the past. When that happens, progress is held back. I'm frustrated by the negative effects of patterns.

Like most things in life, patterns need continuous monitoring and evolution. The lack of which we find the world trying to 'tell', 'allow', and decide for 'Umas'. We try to dictate to them what we think is appropriate.

My wife and I had to establish our own patterns as we began a family. We decided that, for my son's busy years with school and sports, my wife would try to be a local anchor with minimum work travel. To be clear, my wife is much more talented than me and has a very responsible job outside of the home. The decision, however, was not gender-based but based on several practical considerations and it was decided as a team. We both feel pretty good about it.

Now that I am thinking, how is it different from societal patterns in the nineteen fifties? There were barely enough jobs for one adult per family, and contraception was not popular or available; hence, society decided the easiest way was to have men go out and women stay home. We can still argue why society decided to create a pattern with men for outdoor work and women for home. That was a pattern that, at least on some accounts, worked well. We can also argue that in the 1960s, the younger generations purposely broke the boundaries of that pattern. Instead, they created new patterns that often shattered the expectations of the old pattern's faithful. By the 2000s, new generations were challenging those 1960s patterns. The cycle of change continues. The only pattern that is reliable is a pattern of change. People will continue to break patterns that do not fit their needs. In the process, there will be a conflict between those creating change and those demanding obedience to the old pattern. The pattern of Obedience – Conflict – Change is a never-ending cycle. The cycle continues. When Uma was a young adult, she was ready for a new life outside the home, yet most around her were not.

How is it different from businesses? Kodak, despite creating the digital camera technology, still stuck to the various revenue streams of the paper cameras. They refused to break their patterns even when they held innovative technologies. That seems so misguided, just as refusing to alter our social patterns.

I wonder how, in the 1990s in India, Uma could not consider her daughter to be part of their construction business, where ninety-five percent of half-educated men dominated the space? Why were they so blind to the possibilities? What prevented them from seeing Uma's daughter's potential?

Then I look at my own life and see my own blindness. Recently, I enjoyed a lovely steak when I visited Palm Springs. I was surprised when the chef came to my table and introduced herself. I learned she had moved from New York, and I was delighted for her. I felt joy because seeing her answered an age-old question for me. Growing up, I always saw the women cooking, and there were some really great cooks among my aunts and friends' moms.

As soon as I began dining in restaurants, I only saw male cooks. Even today, most chefs are men, yet more than 80% of households in this world are regularly fed by women's cooking. If women do most of the cooking, why are there not more female chefs?

Our household is slightly different; mostly, men cook our food. Not because I cook a greater number of days than my wife, but because we order in through DoorDash and others most days. It is easy to say we cook when we only place an order.

But some men do cook. I am very proud of Uma's son, who loves to cook. He is a great cook, evidently inheriting more of his mother's cooking acumen and interest than his sister. I have no problem with that and consider it very cool. I wish I could enjoy cooking like him.

It is not just in the past. There were patterns in the past, in the present, and there will be patterns in the future. The question is, how do we evolve in a timely manner and not let patterns imprison us in our thinking and decisions?

The problem lies in our response to outdated patterns. By taking too long to break the pattern, we waste talent. We also fail to see the true diversity of passion, willingness and capability, which often comes in a different form than gender and skin colour. We let our biases based on patterns guide our listening and observation skills.

My mom was my maths tutor at home from my early days up to my high school. When I started excelling in mathematics, no one ever made that connection. Everyone assumed my dad was teaching me mathematics at home or some other maths tutor. After all, men are supposed to be naturally better at maths and science. Despite my mom being a language student, she was a homemaker, spending the majority of her time cooking and cleaning. No one expected her to have an aptitude for maths. I mentioned this anecdote in my other publications as well. I will probably find a way to weave this into my future books if the opportunity presents itself. Thank you, mother.

Uma was the mastermind and the most enterprising soul, the savvy businesswoman of her household. The world prefers to know her as a mom, fantastic cook, and grandmom who never worked outside.

Patterns often lull us to sleep, distracting us from noticing what is happening around us. The conversations about patterns caused me to not notice walking through the airport. Suddenly, I looked around the airport as I started walking from my gate towards the doors to my red bus. Most people were busy taking calls. Often, I observe anxious faces when the call is probably not going as well. I am sure I am uptight on my calls sometimes too. Work is integrated. Not just from home or office. Working from everywhere and wherever makes sense. I personally do not see anything wrong with this, as life and work are absolutely integrated as far as I am concerned. Anyways, there were most of the folks wired up and working away or running towards work and pulling their carry-on luggage as if they are in a hundred-metre 'pull your carry-on' race of some kind.

This is the pattern of business travel.

A full generation of the workforce was told in the nineties that multitasking is a superpower, and since then, this generation has been running with the S&P 500 to make progress by doing more faster, trying to juggle all the time. A generation that is on calls all day and half the time semi-present. I detect another pattern that needs to be examined.

Meanwhile, there were others who were not rushing and were slowly and safely heading out of the gate towards the doors. Some of them were on vacation, and others were retired. Maybe even some of the business travellers have figured out the value of being present in the moment.

Looking beyond this sea of travellers, I wonder, "Are some of them staying at home like Uma? Since they stay at home, are they less capable? Or has someone else decided their destiny?"

I continued to wonder, "How many of those always-wired professionals are really meant to be there? How many of them are doing it happily or doing a chore?" Thinking of Uma and her story, I reconsider several of the business and domestic patterns that I have blindly accepted throughout my life.

I wonder, am I following Uma's example by questioning the patterns?

We had an older lady driving the Avis bus today. Should I assume she is a mom and not able to make enough financial freedom and that's why she's earning every bit she can? Or is she a multi-millionaire doing this for fun?

The question continues and a recent memory surfaces.

I was in Napa a couple of months back. An older gentleman cleanly suited was driving me from San Francisco airport to Napa. We exchanged pleasantries and discussed a variety of topics. He was a very engaging person. I have found that it typically takes a couple of hours to travel from the airport to my destination in Napa. I used that time to make several work calls. But because this driver was so engaging, I kept talking to him and put aside my calls. To my surprise, I learned he was a successful corporate executive, higher up in the corporate ladder. He had worked and lived in multiple countries, and now drives for a rental car company because he loves driving and meeting new people. Had I clung to my established patterns, I would not have known this or gotten to know him. This experience convinced me that I needed to be more present and have a rich conversation with him to satisfy his purpose of gracefully contributing to the workforce. I learned a variety of things. I never got permission from him to share his name and stories. Hence, I will not do so here in any further detail. I wish I had asked for his permission. Stories were from various parts of the world and of diverse types.

The two hours just passed.

Patterns are inevitable. The world is full of patterns. Some are created for survival. Some are created for consumerism. They all have or at least had a purpose in the context of society at the point of creation. When we live with these for years, we create a bias towards the patterns.

Biases work against any force that tries to change the patterns. Uma's daughter cannot be seen at a large table where she is the only educated female sitting in the middle of the rest of the middle-aged, barely educated males.

They hold back evolution, dreams, and aspirations until the patterns are broken.

With these random thoughts in mind, following the instructions on the board, I picked up my white Ford Explorer. I set up my Android Play and put up the Google map and headed towards the highway. It was about nine o'clock in India, the end of the day for Uma. I decided to call her to talk about her day.

First Day At Work

I asked Google to call Uma at home using the hands-free in the car. I was a bit anxious as the phone started ringing. If it is already too late, I might be waking her up.

This time, Uma picked up right away as if she was waiting for my call. I asked, "How was your day?" She said, "Very good, it was busy." She sounded different. The tone and the answer were definitely different from any conversation I had with her over the last few years. She sounded a bit tired but excited. Felt like she had a lot to share.

I was trying to distinguish the difference in tone. I think her tone lately suggested 'today was a repetition of yesterday and tomorrow will be of today'. I was not sure if I had asked Uma about her day in many years. I would have asked, "How are you?" in a generic way without really expecting to hear anything specific. I was nice and so was Uma. After Uma's short answer and as soon as she asked about me, the rest of the conversation turned to my life, my travel, my books, my plans and so on. Even if the topic stayed on Uma, it's eighty percent about her grandkids, husband, and kids. For one thing, her husband is no longer with her in this world.

Since I was thinking about this for the last twenty-four hours, I said, "This was your first day at work, right?". Taking a very brief pause, "I have been to the office and participated in various events since I was a three-year-old. Ha ha."

She took another long pause. I did not mean to offend her. I'm not sure if I have inadvertently stepped into something. I was a bit worried.

"But today is the first full day formally, yes." "Yes, I am the principal and owner of the school now. Did you know that? Ha ha," Uma said.

Before I could say anything, she continued, "I will be drawing a salary every month. I guess I joined the workforce, finally."

That was an interesting point. Uma will be paid for work going forward. What about the last 50 years? Was there any back pay for the work she had done? I wondered, what does 'workforce' mean?

I immediately thought about my mom. Forty years of service inside the house. What was her contribution to GDP? How do we ever measure that?

All those meals, all that tutoring my mom did for me and my sister, all that cleaning, all that coaching she did – is that work?

I was searching on the internet to find out the actual number of adults who are homemakers and how we calculate their contribution to the GDP. This is a grey area. I can easily conclude that more than a couple of billion people in the world are homemakers. They are contributing to society and the economy. We just do not have a good way of measuring it. My gratitude goes out to them, like my mom.

Within these thoughts, I wonder when we will break this pattern. How long will it be before we create a pattern that acknowledges the previously invisible contribution of the stay-at-home mom (or dad)? I quickly realised that I needed to listen. As Uma continued, "I spent a few hours with the teachers, made sure their work is evenly allocated, asked them to plan their vacations in advance so that we have enough coverage always." We also created a roster with backup names for each teacher, should anyone fall sick or have to take an unplanned leave. It looks like a list. They created it on the computer and we pasted it on the wall of the teachers' room."

Uma was explaining in simple words. I am guessing some Excel printout on the green wall in the teachers' room. I have been to the teachers' room. It is pretty big, bright and nice. The colours in that room and all the rooms in that school are very lively. As far as I can remember, there was a soft board on the wall where notices and other paper announcements for teachers could be posted with board pins. Uma's husband was a retired engineer and construction entrepreneur. He gave time and attention to details in building the rooms in the school.

Uma went on, "I asked Tamal to keep track of all the fees and make sure we follow up before and after the due dates in case there are delays". Tamal is their accountant, office administrator, and all-in-one. Uma said, "Historically, they only followed up with parents once the due dates passed".

She wanted to make sure I understood the improvement. The previous regime under her husband always followed up if and when the due dates passed. Uma decided to start a system of sending nudges two days before the due date. Uma added, "I suggested an early nudge follow-up two working days before the due date by a reminder letter," Uma said proudly.

I believe she meant an email reminder two days before the due date so that delays decrease overall. I could not help but think about the optimisation of the cash conversion cycle project it was involved in last year. I did not want to stop her flow. Typically, the conversation would have switched to me a long time ago. She would have asked where I was travelling this time, when I would be back home and so on. Not today. This is her day.

Without a pause, Uma said, "Today, about fifty percent of parents pay the fees after the due date." Uma answered exactly the question I was going to ask next about the size of the problem. I had a few more questions about how much pay one week after versus longer delays. Before I could ask the follow-up questions, Uma moved on to the next topic. She is on a roll. She went on. "There is a logistics problem every morning; traffic congestion occurs every morning in front of the building during drop-in hours. Some parents get delayed for work, and the neighbours are also complaining."

I got a chance this time to ask, "What is the cause and how will you solve it?" I added two questions in one. Maybe I was not sure if I would get a chance before the next topic. Uma promptly said, "We figured out the reason and it will be addressed from tomorrow. Some parents just sit and chat in the waiting area with other parents who are obviously not in a rush."

I snuck in my question again, "How does their chatting in the waiting area cause traffic issues?"

Uma responded, "Their vehicles are parked longer in front of the building, which causes the issue."

I curiously asked, "What are you going to do?"

Uma, "Already done, we closed the front door of the waiting area. It will only be used for parent's teacher meetings and other appointments for parents to wait, but will not be kept wide open, particularly during the drop-off and pick-up hours."

While Uma continued with enthusiasm, I could not stop myself from thinking about strategic priorities for my department for this year: succession planning, structural cost management, working capital optimisation, alignment with customer objectives, and so on. We took a few weeks to come up with those thoughts thoughtfully and define a work plan. Obviously, it is a much different scale and context. Still, I could not overlook the similarity of our strategic plan with Uma's course of action on day one.

She probably does not know the term 'working capital', nor does she know about 'succession planning' or 'sustainable operations'. Interestingly enough, her actions positively impacted all three on the very first day.

Common sense and curiosity are such important characteristics of leadership. It is very hard to write in a job description to highlight that requirement - 'person with common sense should only apply.' Common sense is not that common, actually.

Uma, "Are you listening?" I said. "Yes, yes," I might have missed a few things as I drifted into my thoughts.

Uma said, "Independence Day is coming; we will bring a cake, there will be a ceremony, we will hoist the national flag and I will chair the event." "Our councillor will join as well, and the parents are also invited," Uma quickly added, "also grandparents are invited."

I wanted to ask, "Are you missing your husband? Are you able to handle everything by yourselves? How is your health?"

I did not.

Uma continued, explaining the pattern she was creating to invigorate the young minds in her school.

When I interact with university students, particularly in their final year, I always get energised. They are ready to jump into the industry and make a difference. A huge amount of positive energy. Confidence to tackle everything in a fresh and pure way wrapped in a strong belief system. I tell them my story, share some learnings along the way in the form of stories. I hope they get some value out of that. But in reality, I take away much more from those conversations. My mindset gets a 'growth upgrade', as does my optimism for the future. I just feel happier.

Today's conversation with Uma felt quite similar. I felt like I was getting a mindset upgrade. I felt that a super-talented professional had just entered her field of interest, engaged, curious, and committed.

She took a pause and took a sip of water. "We will also revive the library in the school," Uma said. "I used to buy lots of books in advance for my daughter. I never insisted on her to read. As she got surrounded by my books, she started picking up one and then the other, and soon before I realised, she became a voracious reader."

She continued, "I will discuss the idea of a library room with the teachers tomorrow."

The visual of her daughter's room came to mind again. Very tall walls and every inch of the walls except the doors is covered with books. I was thinking of the potential of a library room where the kids are just exploring and reading or browsing books. A room with no tablets or electronics, all tactile paper books. I heard Uma chuckling.

Uma chuckled and said, "I could not become a teacher, but I finally became the principal."

The sound of a chuckle was musical. A fusion of the sounds of joy, achievement, and enthusiasm.

"Uma, are you there? Or have we got disconnected?" I said, "I am here. Congratulations! You are the teacher of the teachers."

Every time for the last ten years, I have closed the conversation by saying, "Take care of your health." Today, I said, "Good night. You have to go to work tomorrow. Have a great second day at work."

About the Author

Debasis "DB" Bhaumik is an entrepreneurial leader who has worked with and for many global Fortune 100 organisations across Asia-Pacific, Europe, and North America. He started his career as a technology entrepreneur in India and has undertaken various leadership roles in North America. He is a well-respected leader, author, speaker, and Board Member.

DB's past books include 'Leadership 4.0: Proven Habits for Sustainable Success in the Digital World', which is based on the belief that technology is a commodity - people are the differentiators; 'Let's Do It Right: A Journey from Exclusion to Inclusion', which is based on the belief that inclusion is powerful as long as the majority is not left behind; and 'Amour: Being in Love' - a couple's relationship journey.